11+ Non-verbal Reasoning

WORKBOOK 1

Non-verbal Reasoning Technique

Dr Stephen C Curran

Edited by Dr Tandip Singh Mann and Andrea Richardson

This book belongs to

Accelerated Education Publications Ltd

Contents

Pages

1. Elements

1.	Shapes	3-7
2.	Fills	8-11
3.	Lines	12-15
4.	Key Questions used in Non-verbal Reasoning	16-19

2. Movements

1.	Reflection	20-22
2.	Rotation	23-25
3.	Inversion	26-28
4.	Superimposition	29-31
5.	Transposition	32-34

3. Manipulations

1.	Size	35-37
2.	Transformation	38-40
3.	Addition	41-43
4.	Subtraction	44-46
5.	Frequency (Counting)	47-49

4. Patterns

1.	Repetition	50-52
2.	Cumulation	53-55

5. Layering

1.	Level One	56-58
2.	Level Two	59-61
3.	Level Three	62-64
4.	Level Four	65-67
5.	Level Five	68-70

© 2006 Stephen Curran

Chapter One
ELEMENTS

Non-verbal Reasoning questions combine three **Elements**:
Shapes • Fills • Lines

1. Shapes
a. Standard Palette

This comprises all 'closed' geometrically defined shapes.
Triangles • Quadrilaterals • Polygons • Circles

(i) Triangles

(iv) Circular Shapes

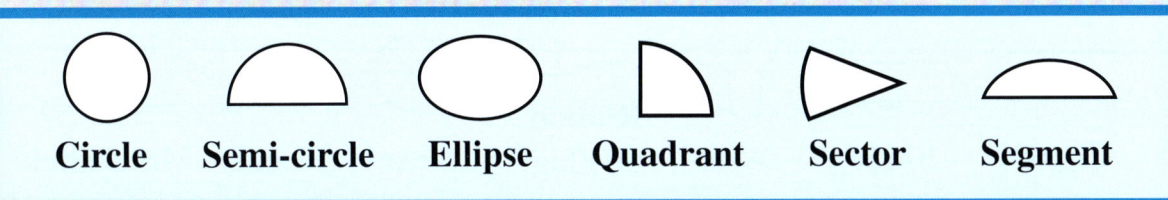

(v) Irregular Polygons

Irregular shapes have unequal sides and angles.

General Quadrilateral   Pentagon   Hexagon

b. Specialist Palette

This comprises everyday recognisable 'closed' shapes.
Straight Shapes • **Curved Shapes**
Other shapes could be shown that are not in these palettes.

(i) Straight Shapes

(ii) Curved Shapes

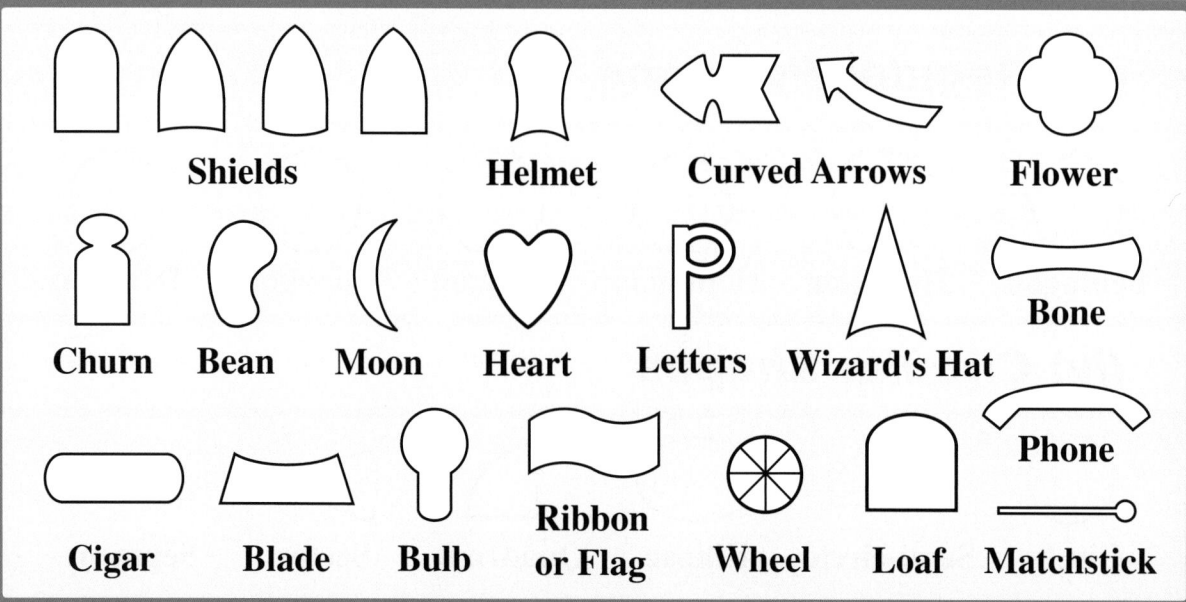

c. Naming Shapes

It is important in Non-verbal Reasoning questions to be able to identify and give **Names to Shapes**. It is much easier to describe what is happening to a shape if it is given a name.

(i) Standard Shapes

Exercise 1: 1   Name the following shapes:

Record scores out of ten here

(ii) Specialist Shapes

Exercise 1: 2   Name the following shapes:

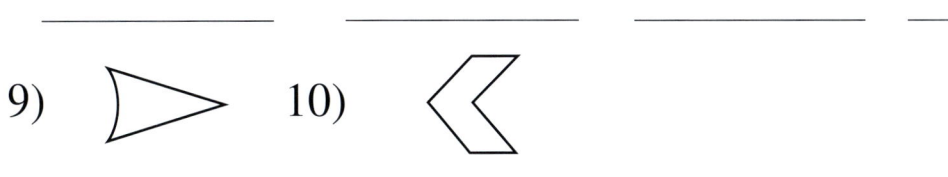

Score

d. Shape Questions

Exercise 1: 3   Answer the following:

1) Which is the next shape in the series?

Answer ___   This shape is called a(n) _____.

2) Which shape does not fit in with the others?

Answer ___   This shape is called a(n) _____.

3) Which shape belongs to this family of shapes?

Answer ___   This shape is called a(n) _____.

4) Which shape is most like the Test Shape?

Answer ___   This shape is called a(n) _____.

5) Which shape is the odd one out?

Answer ___

This shape is called a(n) _____.

6) Which shape does not fit in with these shapes?

a b c d e

Answer ____ This shape is called a(n) _____.

7) Which shape belongs to this family of shapes?

a b
c d

Answer ____ This shape is called a(n) _____.

8) Which shape does not fit in with the others?

a b c d e

Answer ____ This shape is called a(n) _____.

9) Which is the next shape in the series?

a b
c d

Answer ____ This shape is called a(n) _____.

10) Which shape does not fit in with the other shapes?

a b c d e

Answer ____ This shape is called a(n) _____.

Score

2. Fills
a. Fill Categories

'Closed' shape **Fills** comprise five different categories:
Block • Shaded • Cross-hatched • Liquid • Dotted

b. Fill Palette
(i) Block Fills

Black   Grey   White

(ii) Shaded Fills

Horizontal Solid Line | Right Slant Solid Line | Vertical Solid Line | Left Slant Solid Line

Horizontal Dashed Line | Right Slant Dashed Line | Vertical Dashed Line | Left Slant Dashed Line

(iii) Cross-hatched Fills

Squares   Lattice

(iv) Liquid Fills

Speckled | Mottled

(v) Dotted Fills

Close | Spaced

© 2006 Stephen Curran

c. Naming Fills

Giving **Names to Fills** also helps when describing shapes.

Exercise 1: 4   Name the following fills:

1)

Fill category: __Block__
Fill type: _____

2)

Fill category: _____
Fill type: __Lattice__

3)

Fill category: _____
Fill type: _____

4)

Fill category: _____
Fill type: _____

5)

Fill category: _____
Fill type: _____

6)

Fill category: _____
Fill type: _____

7)

Fill category: _____
Fill type: _____

8)

Fill category: _____
Fill type: _____

9)

Fill category: _____
Fill type: _____

10)

Fill category: _____
Fill type: _____

Score

d. Fill Questions

Exercise 1: 5   Answer the following:

1) Which shape is next in the series?

Answer ____
Fill category: _____ Fill type: _____

2) Which shape does not fit in with the others?

Answer ____
Fill category: _____ Fill type: _____

3) Which shape is next in the series?

Answer ____
Fill category: _____ Fill type: _____

4) Which shape does not fit in with the others?

Answer ____
Fill category: _____ Fill type: _____

5) Which shape is next in the series?

Answer ____
Fill category: _____ Fill type: _____

6) Which two shapes are most alike?

Answer ____ and ____

a b c d e

Fill category: _____ Fill type: _____

7) Which shape is the odd one out?

Answer ____

a b c d e

Fill category: _____ Fill type: _____

8) Which shape is most like the Test Shape?

Test Shape   a b c d e

Answer ____

Fill category: _____
Fill type: _____

9) Which is the next shape in the series?

Answer ____

a b c d

Fill category: _____ Fill type: _____

10) Which shape is most like the Test Shape?

Test Shape   a b c d e

Answer ____

Fill category: _____
Fill type: _____

Score

3. Lines
a. Line Palette

All **Line Types** have three main properties:
1. Solid — Dashed — Dotted
2. Straight — Curved
3. Thin — Thick

For example, this Line Type is described as: **Dotted, Curved, Thick**

b. Line Shape Palette

This comprises everyday recognisable 'open' **Line Shapes**.
Straight Line Shapes • **Curved Line Shapes**
This palette is not exhaustive as other shapes also exist.

(i) Straight Line Shapes

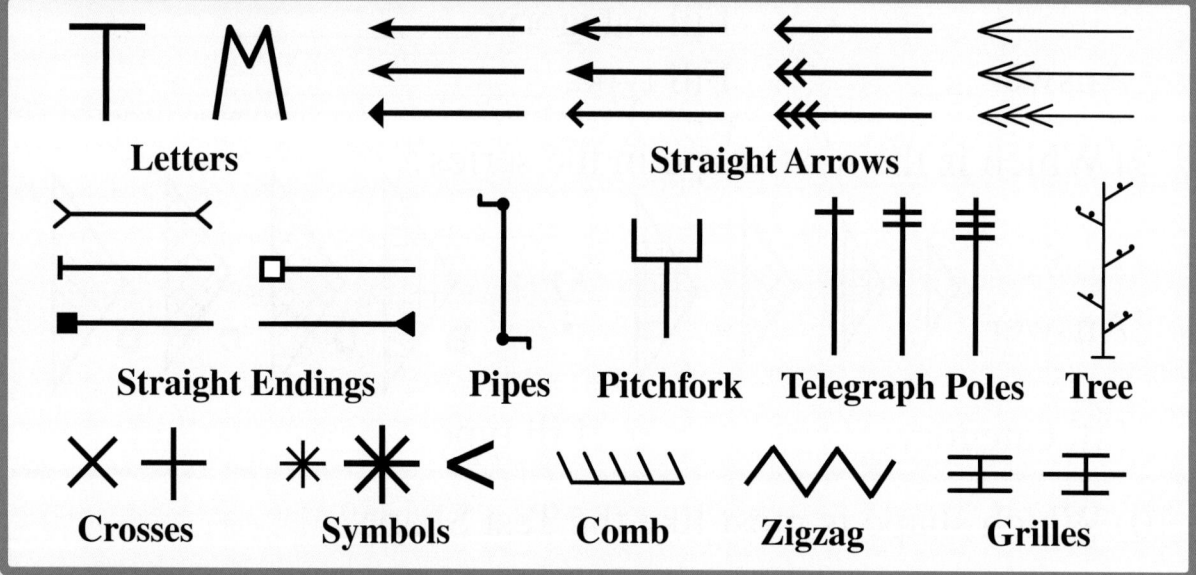

Letters • Straight Arrows
Straight Endings • Pipes • Pitchfork • Telegraph Poles • Tree
Crosses • Symbols • Comb • Zigzag • Grilles

(ii) Curved Line Shapes

Wave • Fish • Basin • Letters
Dots • Curved Arrow • Pulleys • Symbols • Curved Endings

© 2006 Stephen Curran

c. Naming Lines

Naming Lines and Line Shapes helps with identification.

(i) Straight Line Shapes

Exercise 1: 6a Identify the following line types:

1)
Type: Dotted Straight Thin
Shape: _____

2)
Type: _____ _____ _____
Shape: Symbol

3)
Type: _____ _____ _____
Shape: _____

4)
Type: _____ _____ _____
Shape: _____

5)
Type: _____ _____ _____
Shape: _____

(ii) Curved Line Shapes

Exercise 1: 6b Identify the following line types:

6)
Type: _____ _____ _____
Shape: _____

7)
Type: _____ _____ _____
Shape: _____

8)
Type: _____ _____ _____
Shape: _____

9)
Type: _____ _____ _____
Shape: _____

10)
Type: _____ _____ _____
Shape: _____

Score

d. Line Questions

Exercise 1: 7   Answer the following:

1) Which is the next figure in the series?

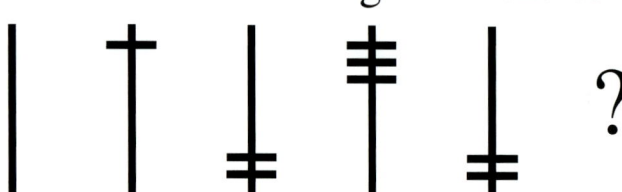

Answer ____   These figures are called _____.

2) Which figure does not fit in with the others?

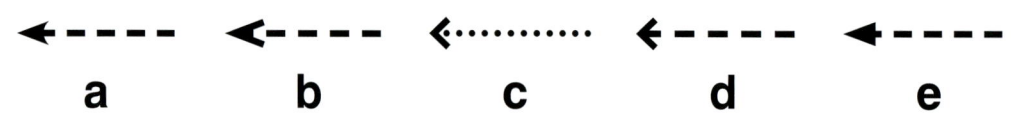

Answer ____   These figures are called _____.

3) Which figure belongs to this family of figures?

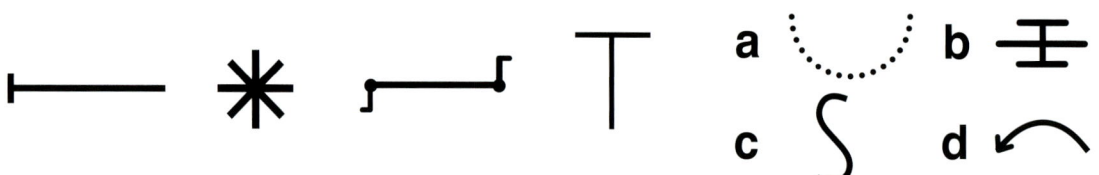

Answer ____   This figure is called a(n) _____.

4) Which figure is most like the Test Figure?

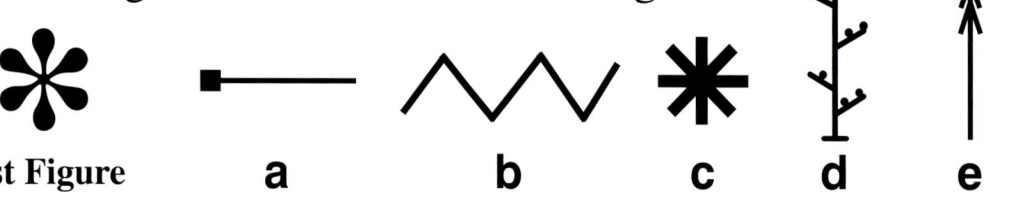

Answer ____   This figure is called a(n) _____.

5) Which figure is the odd one out?

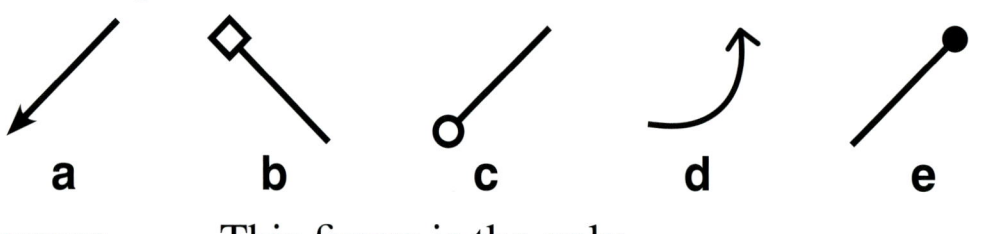

Answer ____   This figure is the only _____.

4. Key Questions used in Non-verbal Reasoning

All Non-verbal Reasoning questions are centred around just three key areas. It is important to be able to identify:

Similarity • Difference • Pattern

These questions have already been used in this book:
1) Which shape is most similar to the shape given?
2) Which shape is most different from the shape given?
3) Which shape is the next shape in the series?

a. Similarity

Shapes are **Similar** if they are like each other in some way. This likeness can apply to any aspect of the shape or shapes.

These two shapes are identical, except they are of a different size and fill type. The second shape has also been rotated 45° in a Clockwise direction in relation to the first shape.

Similarity involves identifying one or more common characteristics between shapes.

Example: Which shape is most similar to the Test Shape?

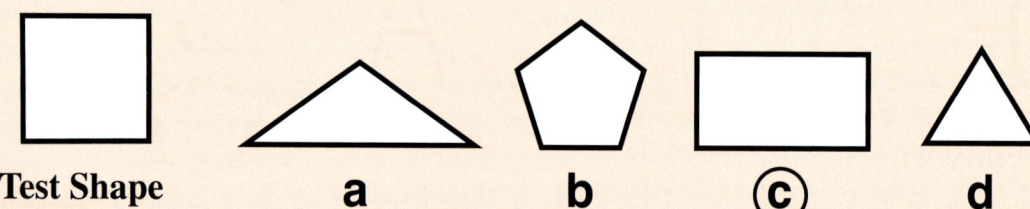

Answer: Shape **c** is most similar as it has four sides.

b. Difference

Shapes are **Different** if they are unlike each other in some way. Difference can mean the shape or shapes have no likeness at all, or there are one or more aspects not alike.

Both these shapes are Stars with the same fill type but they have a different number of sides.

Difference involves spotting the shape most unlike the rest.

Example: Which shape is different from the other shapes?

Answer: Shape **d** is different because it has a Black Fill.

c. Pattern

A **Repetitive** or **Cumulative Pattern** can be established in a series or sequence of shapes or figures (see pages 50-55).

The fill changes from Grey to White to Grey repetitively. One more Circle with a Black Fill is added each time cumulatively.

A pattern is identified by spotting repetition or cumulation.

Example: Which shape is next in the series?

Answer: Shape **c** is next because it is bigger and it has a White Fill.

Exercise 1: 8   Answer the following:

1) Which is the next shape in the series?

Answer ____   Why? _____

2) Which shape does not fit in with the others?

a   b   c   d   e

Answer ____   Why not? _____

3) Which shape is next in the series?

Answer ____   Why? _____

4) Which shape does not fit in with the others?

a   b   c   d   e

Answer ____   Why not? _____

5) Which is the next shape in the series?

Answer ____   Why? _____

6) Which two shapes are most alike?

a   b   c   d   e

Answer ____ and ____   Why? _____
_____

7) Which shape is the odd one out?

a   b   c   d   e

Answer ____   Why? _____
_____

8) Which shape is most similar to the Test Shape?

Test Shape   a   b   c   d   e

Answer ____   Why? _____
_____

9) Which shape is next in the series?

a   b
c   d

Answer ____   Why? _____
_____

10) Which shape is most like the Test Shape?

Test Shape   a   b   c   d   e

Score

Answer ____   Why? _____
_____

© 2006 Stephen Curran

Chapter Two
MOVEMENTS

In Non-verbal Reasoning, shapes can **Move** in five ways:
**Reflection • Rotation • Inversion
Superimposition • Transposition**

1. Reflection

A shape can be **Reflected** across an imaginary Mirror Line or Line of Reflection. Shape **A** is reflected the other side of the Mirror Line to form shape **B**.

Key Non-verbal Reasoning questions apply to reflections:

Example 1: Which shape is a reflection of the Test Shape?

Test Shape   a   b   ⓒ   d   e

Answer: **c** is a reflection of the Test Shape.

Example 2: Which pair of shapes are not reflections?

a   ⓑ   c   d

Answer: **b** - The Slanted Shaded Fills are not reflections.

Example 3: Which is the next shape in the series?

a   b   ⓒ   d

Answer: **c** - The shape reflects correctly and has the correct Liquid Fill type.

Exercise 2: 1   Answer the following:

1) Which is the next figure in the series?

Answer ____   Fill category: _____
                Fill type: _____

2) Which pair of shapes does not fit in with the others?

Answer ____   These shapes are called _____ .

3) Which is the next figure in the series?

                Fill category: _____
Answer ____   Fill type: _____

4) Which figure does not fit in with the others?

                Why not? _____
Answer ____   _____

5) Which letter is next in the series?

Y A C D E H I ?   a L   b K
                   c M   d B

Answer ____ Why? _____
_____

© 2006 Stephen Curran

6) Which two pairs of shapes are most alike?

a   b   c   d   e

Answer ____ and ____   Why? _____

7) Which pair of shapes is the odd one out?

a   b   c   d   e

Answer ____   i) Why? _____
ii) These shapes are called _____.

8) Which figure is a reflection of the Test Figure?

Test Figure   a   b   c   d   e

Answer ____   The inner shape is called a(n) _____.

9) Which is the next shape in the series?

a   b   c   d

What is this shape called?

Answer ____ _____

10) Which figure is a reflection of the Test Figure?

Test Figure   a   b   c   d   e

Answer ____   The outer shape is called a(n) _____.

Score ____

2. Rotation

In Non-verbal Reasoning, shapes can **Rotate** in a Clockwise or Anticlockwise direction.

To avoid confusion it is best to measure the rotation by the shortest route. This will be in either a **Clockwise** or an **Anticlockwise** direction around the **360°** turn. There are three main rotations:

$45° (\frac{1}{8})$ turn $90° (\frac{1}{4})$ turn $180° (\frac{1}{2})$ turn

Smaller shapes can rotate around the outside of larger shapes or on the inside of larger shapes.

The Pencil Shape has moved Anticlockwise around the Pentagon and the Circle has moved Clockwise within the Pentagon.

Key Non-verbal Reasoning questions apply to rotations:

Example 1: Which shape completes the second pair of shapes?

Answer: **c** - It has rotated 90° Clockwise (in the same way as the first pair).

Example 2: Which rotation is the odd one out?

Answer: **d** - It has rotated 90° Anticlockwise but should rotate 180°.

Example 3: Which figure is next in the series?

Answer: **d** - The Arrow rotates 45° Anticlockwise; the next Arrow must have a Black Fill; the Circle rotates 45° Clockwise around the centre (or 90° Clockwise around the Arrow).

Exercise 2: 2   Answer the following:

1) Which is the next figure in the series?

Answer ____   The Hexagon has been rotated Clockwise ____°.

The Ellipse rotates around the Hexagon in a(n) _____ direction.

2) Which pair of shapes does not rotate like the Test Shapes?

Test Shapes   a   b   c

Answer ____   The shape has been rotated ____°.

3) Which shape rotates in the same way as the Test Shapes?

Test Shapes   a   b   c

Answer ____   The shape has been rotated ____° _____.

4) Which figure is most like the Test Figure?

Test Figure   a   b   c   d

Answer ____   In comparison with the outer shape the inner shapes have rotated ____° and ____°.

5) Which figure is the odd one out?

a   b   c   d   e

Answer ____   It rotates in a(n) _____ direction.

6) Which figure does not fit in with the other figures?

Answer ____ Why not? _____

7) Which shape belongs to this family of shapes?

Why? _____
Answer ____ _____

8) Which pair of shapes does not rotate like the Test Shapes?

Test Shapes   a   b   c

Answer ____ This shape has been rotated ____°.

9) Which figure is next in the series?

Answer ____ The Flower Shape rotates ____°.
The Moon Shape rotates ____° _____ around the Flower.

10) Which letter is missing from this family of letters?

D E G J K L M

a F   b N
c O   d H

Answer ____ Why? _____
_____

Score

© 2006 Stephen Curran

25

3. Inversion

In Non-verbal Reasoning, a shape can be **Inverted** (Flipped) Horizontally or Vertically or in both directions at the same time:

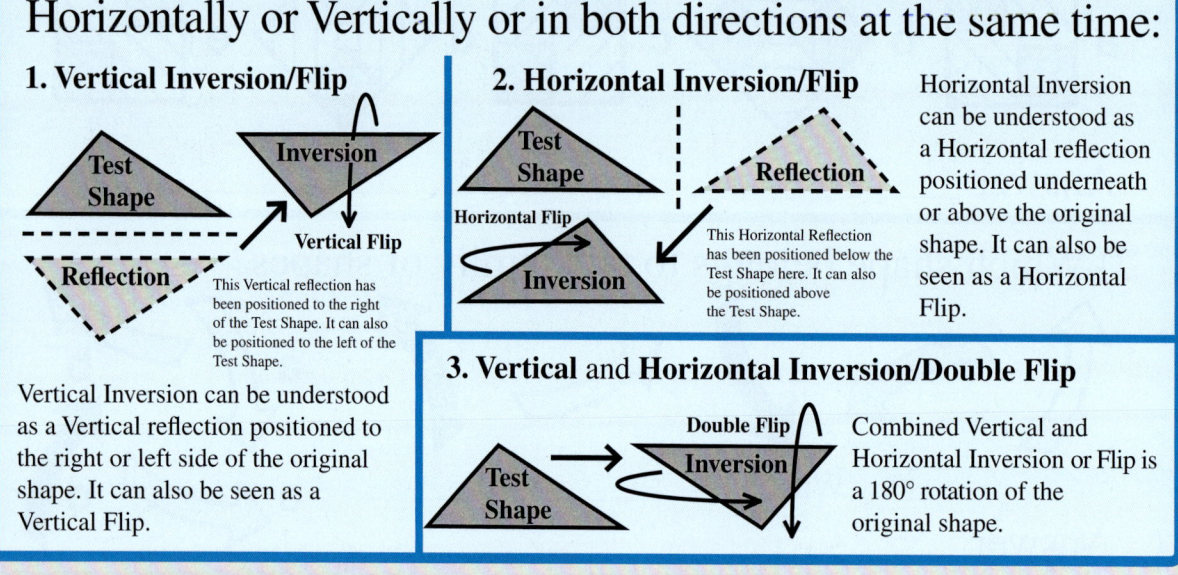

1. Vertical Inversion/Flip

This Vertical reflection has been positioned to the right of the Test Shape. It can also be positioned to the left of the Test Shape.

Vertical Inversion can be understood as a Vertical reflection positioned to the right or left side of the original shape. It can also be seen as a Vertical Flip.

2. Horizontal Inversion/Flip

This Horizontal Reflection has been positioned below the Test Shape here. It can also be positioned above the Test Shape.

Horizontal Inversion can be understood as a Horizontal reflection positioned underneath or above the original shape. It can also be seen as a Horizontal Flip.

3. Vertical and Horizontal Inversion/Double Flip

Combined Vertical and Horizontal Inversion or Flip is a 180° rotation of the original shape.

Key Non-verbal Reasoning questions apply to inversions:

Example 1: Which figure is most similar to the Test Figure?

Answer: **b** - This is a Horizontal inversion/flip. (Horizontal reflection positioned above the original shape.)

Example 2: Which shape is next in the series?

Answer: **d** - This is a Vertical inversion/flip. (Vertical reflection positioned to the side of the original shape.)

Example 3: Which pair of shapes is the odd one out?

Answer: **d** - This is a Horizontal and Vertical inversion (rotated 180°).

Exercise 2: 3   Answer the following:

1) Which shape is next in the series?

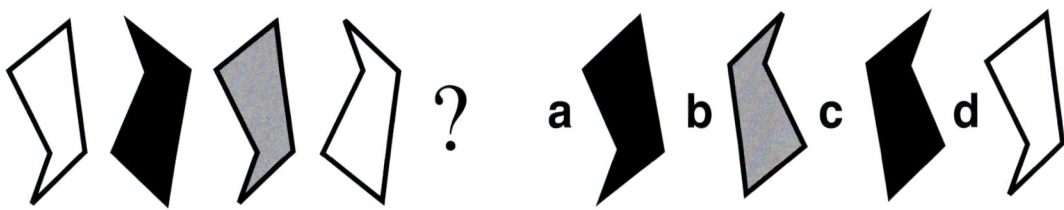

Answer _____   Inversion type? _____ Vertical inversion/flip _____

2) Which shape does not fit in with the others?

Why not? _____

Answer _____

3) Which is the next shape in the series?

Why? _____

Answer _____

4) Which pair of shapes does not fit in with the others?

Why not? _____

Answer _____

5) Which shape is next in the series?

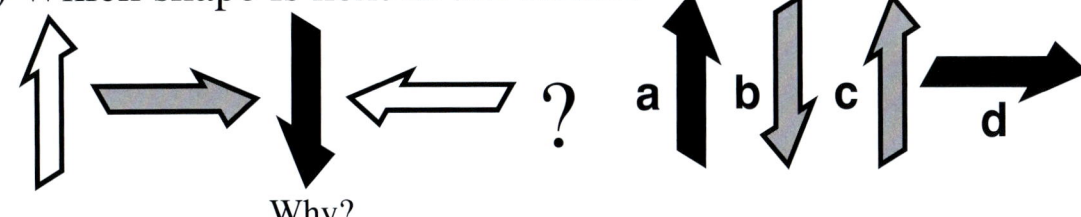

Why? _____

Answer _____

6) Which two shapes are most similar?

a   b   c   d   e

Answer ___ and ___   Why? _____

7) Which figure is the odd one out?

a   b   c   d   e

Answer ___   Why? _____

8) Which figure is most unlike the Test Figure?

Test Figure   a   b   c   d   e

Answer ___   Why? _____

9) Which is the next shape in the series?

?   a   b   c   d

Answer ___   Why? _____

10) Which pair of figures is most like the Test Figures?

Test Figures   a   b   c   d

Answer ___   Why? _____

Score

4. Superimposition

In Non-verbal Reasoning, shapes can be **Superimposed** onto other shapes. These superimpositions can include a **Merger**, an **Overlay**, a **Linkage** or an **Enclosure**.

1. Merger — **2. Overlay** — **3. Linkage** — **4. Enclosure**

| Superimpositions have been indicated with a Grey Fill to help with visual clarity and ease of understanding. | The second shape Merges (crosses over) the first shape. The integrity (lines) of both shapes is retained. In this case it is a 90° rotation and inversion of the original shape. | The second shape Overlays (is on top of) the first shape. The original shape can be fully or partially covered. In this case it is a 90° rotation of the original shape. | The second shape is Linked to (does not cross over) the first shape. The integrity (lines) of both shapes is kept. Several shapes can be Linked together. | The second shape is Enclosed within the first shape. In this case a copy of the first shape is reduced in size and Enclosed within the original shape. |

Key Non-verbal Reasoning questions use superimpositions:

Example 1: Which figure is most similar to the Test Figure?

Test Figure — a — b — c — ⓓ

Answer: **d** - This is a rotated superimposed merger of 90°.

Example 2: Which superimposition is the odd one out?

a — b — ⓒ — d — e

Answer: **c** - The enclosed shape has not been rotated 180°.

Example 3: Which superimposition is next in the series?

Answer: **b** - The previous figure has been rotated 90°. The Cigar Shape with a Grey Fill overlays the Bone Shape.

Exercise 2: 4   Answer the following:

1) Which is the next figure in the series?

Superimposition type:

Answer ____ _____

2) Which figure does not fit in with the others?

Answer ____   Superimposition type: _____

3) Which figure belongs to this family of figures?

Superimposition type: _____

Answer ____

4) Which figure is most like the Test Figure?

Test Figure

Answer ____   Superimposition type: _____

5) Which figure is the odd one out?

Answer ____   Superimposition type: _____

6) Which figure does not fit in with the others?

a   b   c   d

Answer ____
Superimposition types: _____ and _____

7) Which figure belongs to this family of figures?

a   b
c   d

Answer ____   Superimposition type: _____

8) Which figure does not fit in with the other figures?

a   b   c   d   e

Answer ____   Superimposition type: _____

9) Which figure is next in the series?

a   b   c   d

Answer ____   Superimposition type: _____

10) Which figure belongs to this family of figures?

a   b   c   d

Answer ____
Superimposition types: _____ / _____ / _____

Score

5. Transposition

In Non-verbal Reasoning, shapes can be **Transposed** or **Moved** from one position to another, either Horizontally or Vertically. Movements to the right or left are Horizontal, and movements up or down are Vertical. Some transpositions involve both Vertical and Horizontal movements, i.e. a shape could move up and to the right.

Transpositions are enclosed to show movement.

1. Horizontal Transposition
2. Vertical Transposition
3. Horizontal and Vertical Transposition

Key Non-verbal Reasoning questions use transpositions:

Example 1: Which figure is most similar to the Test Figure?

Test Figure   a   ⓑ   c

Answer: **b** - It is a Vertical and Horizontal transposition.

Example 2: Which transposition is the odd one out?

ⓐ   b   c   d

Answer: **a** - It is a Horizontal transposition.

Example 3: Which transposition is next in the series?

Answer: **c** - The Hexagon changes to a Grey Fill and transposes Vertically.

Exercise 2: 5   Answer the following:

1) Which figure is next in the series?

Answer ____   Transposition types:

Grey Fill: _Horizontal_   White: _____   Black: _____

2) Which figure completes the second pair of figures?

Transposition types: Flower: _____

Answer ____   Curved Arrow: _____   Circle: _____

3) Which is the next figure in the series?

Answer ____   Transposition types:
Circle: _____   Pentagon: _____

4) Which pair of figures does not fit in with the others?

Transposition type:

Answer ____   _____ and _____

5) Which is the next figure in the series?

Transposition types:

Answer ____   Octagon: _____   Kite: _____

© 2006 Stephen Curran

6) Which figure completes the second pair of figures?

Answer _____   Transposition types: Curved Arrow: _____
F Shape: _____ and _____

7) Which pair of figures is the odd one out?

Answer _____   Transposition type: _____

8) Which pair of figures is most like the Test Figures?

Answer _____   Transposition types:
Black Shape: _____ Grey Shape: _____

9) Which figure is next in the series?

Answer _____
Transposition type: _____

10) Which pair of figures is most like the Test Figures?

Answer _____
Transposition types:
_____ and _____

Score ____

34   © 2006 Stephen Curran

Chapter Three
MANIPULATIONS

In Non-verbal Reasoning, shapes can be **Manipulated** by:
Size • **Transformation** • **Addition** • **Subtraction** • **Frequency**

1. Size

Shapes can **Increase** in size or **Decrease** in size:

1. Enlargement | **2. Reduction**

Key Non-verbal Reasoning questions apply to size change:

Example 1: Which shape completes the second pair of shapes?

Answer: Shape **e** is a reduction and has a Speckled Fill.

Example 2: Which shape is different from the others?

Answer: Shape **d** is an enlargement of the other shapes.

Example 3: Which shape is next in the series?

Answer: Shape **a** is a reduction (the next smallest) and has the correct fill.

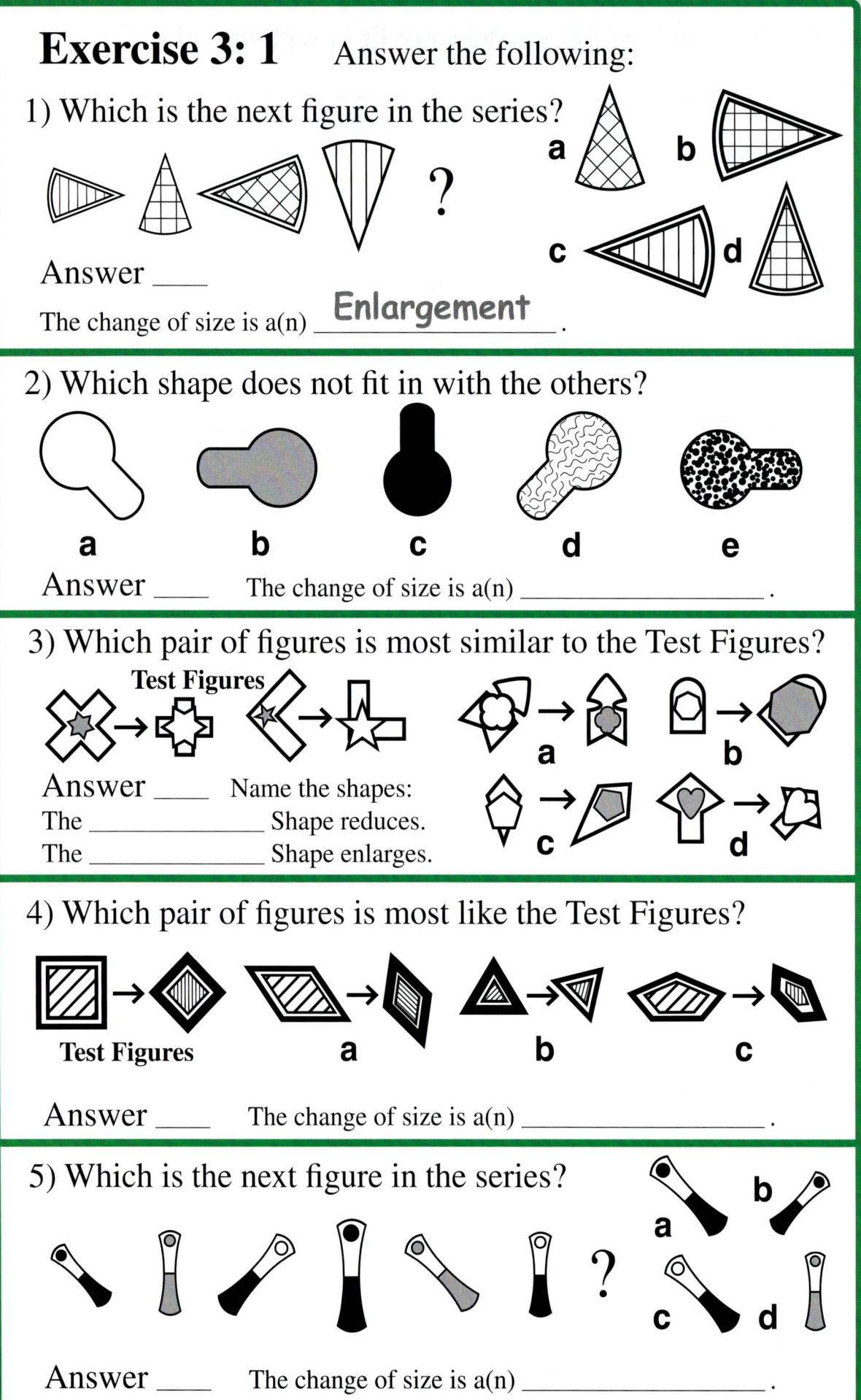

6) Which pair of figures does not fit in with the other figures?

a   b   c   d

Answer _____   The change of size is a(n) _____ .

7) Which figure belongs to this family of figures?

Answer _____

The enclosed shape is a(n) _____ of the outer shape.

8) Which figure does not fit in with the others?

a   b   c   d   e

Answer _____   The change of size is a(n) _____ .

9) Which figure is the odd one out?

a   b   c

Answer _____   The change of size is a(n) _____ .

10) Which figure belongs to this family of figures?

Answer _____

If the enclosed Triangles are placed in size order, largest to smallest, each one would be a(n) _____ of the previous Triangle.

Score

2. Transformation

In Non-verbal Reasoning, shapes can be **Transformed**. This means a shape can be **Stretched** or **Squashed** but retains its main characteristics, i.e. the same number of sides and vertices (corners) and one dimension must remain constant.

1. Stretched   2. Squashed

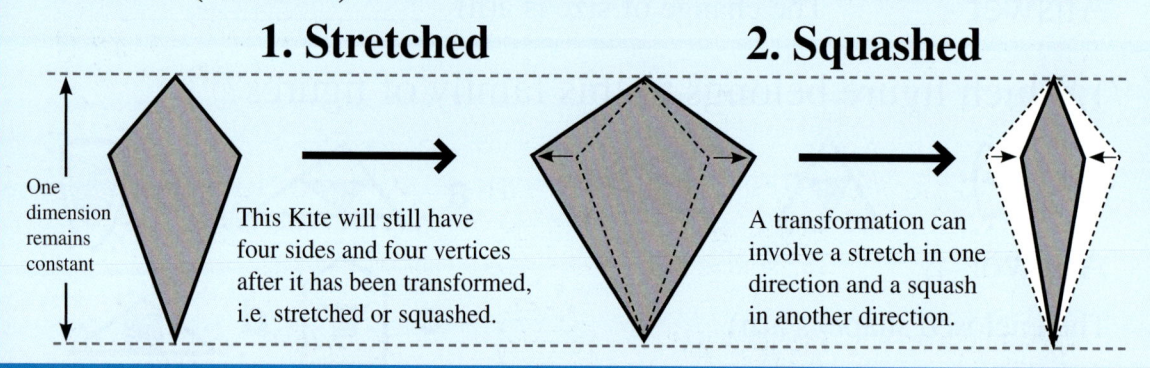

One dimension remains constant

This Kite will still have four sides and four vertices after it has been transformed, i.e. stretched or squashed.

A transformation can involve a stretch in one direction and a squash in another direction.

Key Non-verbal Reasoning questions apply to transformations:

Example 1: Which shape is a transformation of the Test Shape?

Test Shape   a   b   c   ⓓ   e

Answer: **d** is a squashed Parallelogram with a Black Fill.

Example 2: Which pair of shapes are not transformations?

a   b   ⓒ   d

Answer: **c** as the shapes are different and not transformed.

Example 3: Which shape is next in the series?

?   a   ⓑ
     c   d

Answer: **b** has been stretched and has the correct Grey Fill.

38   © 2006 Stephen Curran

Exercise 3: 2 Answer the following:

1) Which is the next figure in the series?

Answer ____
The figure has been __Squashed__ .

2) Which pair of shapes does not fit in with the others?

Answer ____ The shape has been _____ .

3) Which is the next figure in the series?

Answer ____
The House Shape has been _____ .
The Cross Shape has been _____ .

4) Which figure is the odd one out?

Answer ____ The _____ Shape has been squashed.

5) Which figure is next in the series?

Answer ____ The _____ Shape has been stretched.

© 2006 Stephen Curran

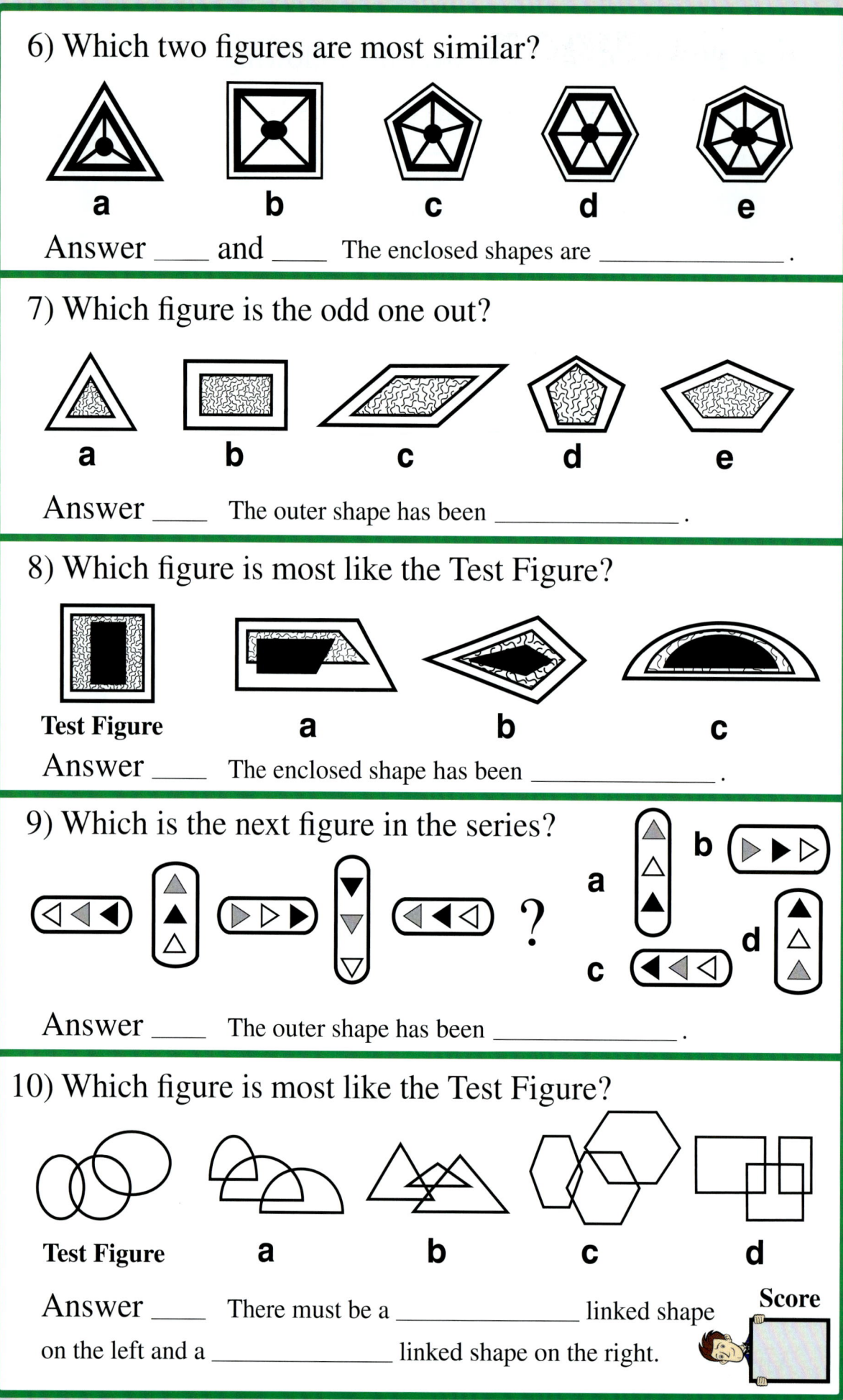

3. Addition

In Non-verbal Reasoning, one or more shapes can be **Added** to the original shape or separate additional shapes can be added.

1. Additions to shapes

The original shape has been copied, rotated 90° and superimposed onto the original shape. Additions are often combined with rotations, reflections, superimpositions and inversions.

2. Additional shapes

A third shape has been added to the two original shapes. This can also be understood as a change in Frequency (see pages 47-49).

Key Non-verbal Reasoning questions apply to additions:

Example 1: Which shape has an addition to the Test Shape?

Test Shape   a   b   ⓒ   d

Answer: **c** - The original shape has received an addition.

Example 2: Which shape has no additions to the Test Shape?

Test Shape   a   ⓑ   c

Answer: **b** - The shape has been rotated but has no additions.

Example 3: Which figure is next in the series?

     ⓐ b

c d

Answer: **a**

This has an addition of one Triangle with a White Fill at the top of the square and one more Circle with a Black Fill in the middle.

Exercise 3: 3   Answer the following:

1) Which is the next figure in the series?

 ?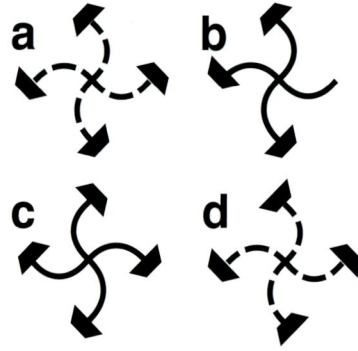

Name the shape that should be added.
Answer ____ _____

2) Which pair of figures does not fit in with the others?

Answer ____ The missing overlay shape is a(n) _____.

3) Which pair of figures belongs to this family of figures?

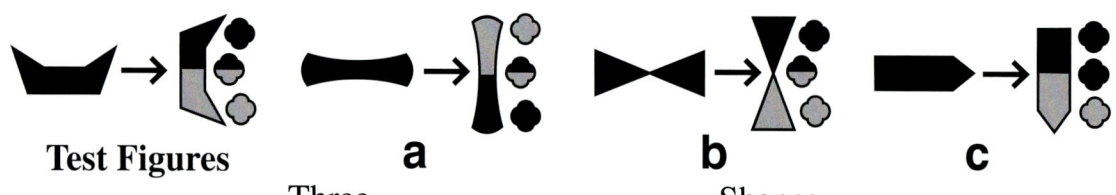

Answer ____
Two linked _____ Shapes
of different sizes must be added.

4) Which pair of figures is most like the Test Figures?

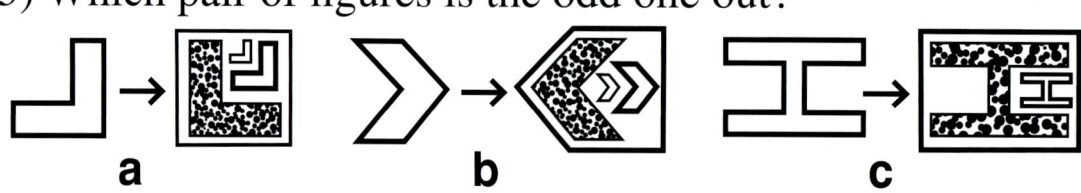

Test Figures

Answer ____ Three _____ Shapes with the correct fills must be added.

5) Which pair of figures is the odd one out?

   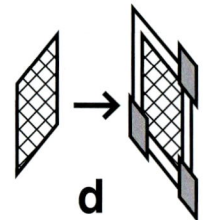

a   b   c

Answer ____ How many smaller shapes should have been added? _____ shape(s)

6) Which pair of figures does not fit in with the other figures?

Answer ____ The added shape should have a _____ fill.

7) Which pair of figures is most like the Test Figures?

Test Figures

Answer ____ How many shapes need to be added? ____ shape(s)

8) Which pair of figures does not fit in with the others?

Answer ____
Why not? _____

9) Which is the next figure in the series?

Answer ____

The correct order of block fills is:
____ ____ ____ ____

10) Which pair of figures belongs to this family of figures?

Answer ____
The three rules are:
i) _____
ii) _____
iii) _____

Score ____

4. Subtraction

In Non-verbal Reasoning, smaller shapes or parts of a shape can be **Subtracted** from the original shape or shapes.

1. Subtracting parts of shapes

The original Kite with a Block Black Fill has had a Triangular section subtracted from it. The shape that remains is an Isosceles Triangle with a Block Black Fill.

2. Subtracting shapes

The Circles with a Speckled Fill and a Block Black Fill have been subtracted from the original group. This can also be understood as a change in Frequency (see pages 47-49).

Key Non-verbal Reasoning questions apply to subtractions:

Example 1: Which shape is a subtraction of the Test Shape?

Test Shape   a   b   ⓒ   d

Answer: **c** - It has a subtraction or missing piece.

Example 2: Which shape is not a subtraction of the Test Shape?

Test Shape   a   b   c   ⓓ

Answer: **d** - This shape has been rotated but it is the same.

Example 3: Which figure is next in the series?

      ?

ⓐ   b

c   d

Answer: **a**

It is a 90° Anticlockwise rotation. The Ribbon Shape with a Block Black Fill is subtracted as it moves to the bottom left of the square.

Exercise 3: 4   Answer the following:

1) Which is the next figure in the series?

Answer _____

A _____ must be subtracted each time in a(n) _____ direction around the shape.

2) Which pair of figures does not fit in with the others?

Answer _____   What two things must be subtracted each time?

i) _____   ii) _____

3) Which figure is next in the series?

What two things must be subtracted?

Answer _____   i) _____   ii) _____

4) Which pair of figures does not fit in with the others?

Why not? _____

Answer _____   _____

5) Which is the next figure in the series?

Answer _____

What is the order of subtraction? (Underline the correct answer.)
Vertical then Horizontal figure **or** Horizontal then Vertical figure.

6) Which two pairs of shapes are most alike?

a b c d

Answer ____ and ____ Which two things must be subtracted each time?
i) _____ ii) _____

7) Which pair of figures is the odd one out?

a b c d

Answer ____ What must be subtracted each time?
_____

8) Which pair of figures is most like the Test Figures?

Test Figures a b c

Which two things must be subtracted?
Answer ____ i) _____ ii) _____

9) Which figure is next in the series?

a b c d

Answer ____

What must be subtracted? _____

10) Which pair of figures is most like the Test Figures?

Test Figures a b c

Answer ____ Which two things must be subtracted?
i) _____
ii) _____

Score ____

© 2006 Stephen Curran

5. Frequency (Counting)

In Non-verbal Reasoning, **Frequency** involves the counting of shapes, smaller shapes within other shapes, or parts of shapes.

1. Counting shapes

The original figure has three Vertical Arrows. The frequency (number) in the second figure is increased to four Horizontal Arrows. **This change could also be understood as an addition.**

2. Counting parts of shapes

The original figure has three Ellipses with a Black Fill. The frequency (number) in the second figure is decreased to two Ellipses with a Black Fill. **This change could also be understood as a subtraction.**

Key Non-verbal Reasoning questions apply to frequency:

Example 1: Which figure is most similar to the Test Figure?

Test Figure   a   b   ⓒ   d

Answer: **c** - It has a frequency of six like the Test Figure.

Example 2: Which figure is most different from the others?

a   b   c   d   ⓔ

Answer: **e** - It has a frequency of six rather than seven.

Example 3: Which figure is next in the series?

a   ⓑ

c   d

Answer: **b**
The frequency (number) of Squares should be eight. The fill types of the Squares are not relevant. The Equilateral Triangle should point upwards and have Vertical Shading.

Exercise 3: 5   Answer the following:

1) Which is the next figure in the series?

Answer ____
Write out the number sequence of the six figures.
It begins with **8,** _____

2) Which figure does not fit in with the others?

Why not? _____
Answer ____

3) Which figure belongs to this family of figures?

Answer ____   There should be _____ enclosures inside the shape.

4) Which pair of figures is most like the Test Figures?

Test Figures

Answer ____   How many 'H' letters should there be? ____

5) Which pair of figures is the odd one out?

Why? _____
Answer ____

48   © 2006 Stephen Curran

6) Which figure does not fit in with the other figures?

a   b   c   d

Why not? _____

Answer ____ _____

7) Which figure belongs to this family of figures?

a   b   c

Answer ____   The enclosed shape should have ____ less sides.

8) Which figure does not fit in with the others?

a   b   c   d   e

Answer ____   There should be ____ of each type of line ending.

9) Which is the next figure in the series?

?   a   b   c   d

Answer ____
Write out the number sequence of the six figures.
It begins with **4**, _____

10) Which figure belongs to this family of figures?

a   b   c

Answer ____   Why? _____
_____

Score

Chapter Four
PATTERNS

In Non-verbal Reasoning, shapes can make **Patterns** in two ways:
Repetition • **Cumulation**

1. Repetition

Shapes can be be arranged in a **Repetitive** pattern:

The Telegraph Poles are in a repetitive pattern of one, two, three, two, one, two, three crossbars, etc.

Key Non-verbal Reasoning questions apply to repetition:

Example 1: Which shape is first in the series?

Answer: **d** - It has the correct shading and rotation.

Example 2: Which shape is missing in the series?

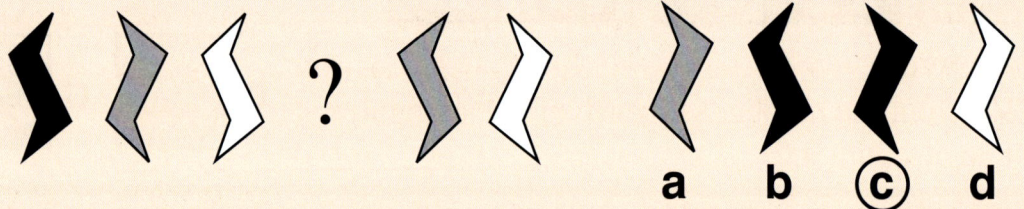

Answer: **c** - It has a Black Fill and is the correct reflection.

Example 3: Which figure is next in the series?

Answer: **c** - Both shapes have the correct fill and rotation.

Exercise 4: 1 Answer the following:

1) Which is the next figure in the series?

Answer ____

Write out the repetitive pattern of the Squares with a Black Fill in numerical terms: _____

2) Which figure is first in the series?

Answer ____ Do the Shaded Fills rotate Clockwise or Anticlockwise? _____

3) Which is the missing figure in the series?

Answer ____ As the shapes are rotated, what kind of movement takes place? _____

4) Which is the next figure in the series?

Answer ____

Write out the order of fills for the Ellipses given in the answer: _____

5) Which figure is first in the series?

Answer ____

Describe the fill of the Triangle in this figure. _____

© 2006 Stephen Curran

6) Which is the missing figure in the series?

Answer ____ Write out the repetitive pattern of the Asterisks in numerical terms: _____

7) Which figure is next in the series?

Answer ____ Which shape is repeated in every other figure of the series? _____

8) Which figure is next in the series?

Answer ____ Write out the order of fills for the Ellipses: _____

9) Which figure is missing in the series?

Answer ____ Describe the three-fold size progression for the Circle:
_____ _____ _____

10) Which is the next figure in the series?

Answer ____
Study the Square Shape.

The Black Fill rotates in a(n) _____ direction.

The Grey Fill rotates in a(n) _____ direction.

2. Cumulation

Shapes can be arranged in a **Cumulative** pattern:

The Pentagon builds side by side in five stages.

Key Non-verbal Reasoning questions apply to cumulation:

Example 1: Which shape is first in the series?

     a

Answer: **b** is a larger shape and has the correct Liquid Fill.

c d

Example 2: Which figure is missing in the series?

a b

c d

Answer: **d** has Pentagons that lie diagonally from bottom left to top right and has a fill order of Black, Grey, Black.

Example 3: Which figure is next in the series?

Answer: **a** has six lines so it is the correct Zigzag Line Shape. It is also the correct direction of the Zigzag Line Shape.

© 2006 Stephen Curran

Exercise 4: 2   Answer the following:

1) Which is the next figure in the series?

Answer _____   Name the three shapes used each time:

_____   _____   _____

2) Which figure is first in the series?

Answer _____   Name the two types of line used:

i) _____   ii) _____

3) Which is the missing figure in the series?

Answer _____   Which shape must be subtracted each time? _____

4) Which is the next figure in the series?

Answer _____   Which shape is cumulative? _____

5) Which figure is first in the series?

Answer _____   Each time, which shape must be:

i) added? _____   ii) subtracted? _____

54   © 2006 Stephen Curran

6) Which is the missing figure in the series?

Answer _____ Which shape is added? _____

7) Which is the next figure in the series?

Answer _____ Name the two cumulative actions:
i) _____
ii) _____

8) Which figure is first in the series?

Answer _____ What must be subtracted? _____

9) Which is the missing figure in the series?

Answer _____ What shape is subtracted? _____

10) Which is the next figure in the series?

Answer _____
Name the repetitive pattern of the fills sequence
of the Squares: _____

The cumulative actions are: _____

Score

© 2006 Stephen Curran

55

Chapter Five
LAYERING

Non-verbal Reasoning questions are complicated by the process of **Layering**. Questions can have up to five layers (or changes) that have to be observed to find a solution.

1. Level One

Some shapes only have one layer or change.

Test Shape

The Segment Shape has received only one layer or change. It has been rotated 180°.

Key Non-verbal Reasoning questions apply to layering:

Example 1: Which shape is most similar to the Test Shape?

Test Shape a b c ⓓ

Answer: **d** is circular, as is the Test Shape.

Example 2: Which shape is most unlike the Test Shape?

Test Shape a b ⓒ d

Answer: **c** has a Black Fill; the Test Shape has a Speckled Fill.

Example 3: Which shape is next in the series?

     ? a ⓑ

Answer: **b** has been rotated 45° in an Anticlockwise direction.

c   d

Exercise 5: 1   Answer the following:

1) Which is the next shape in the series?

Answer ____

2) Which shape does not fit in with the others?

Answer ____

3) Which figure belongs to this family of figures?

Answer ____

4) Which figure is most like the Test Figure?

Test Figure

Answer ____

5) Which shape is the odd one out?

Answer ____

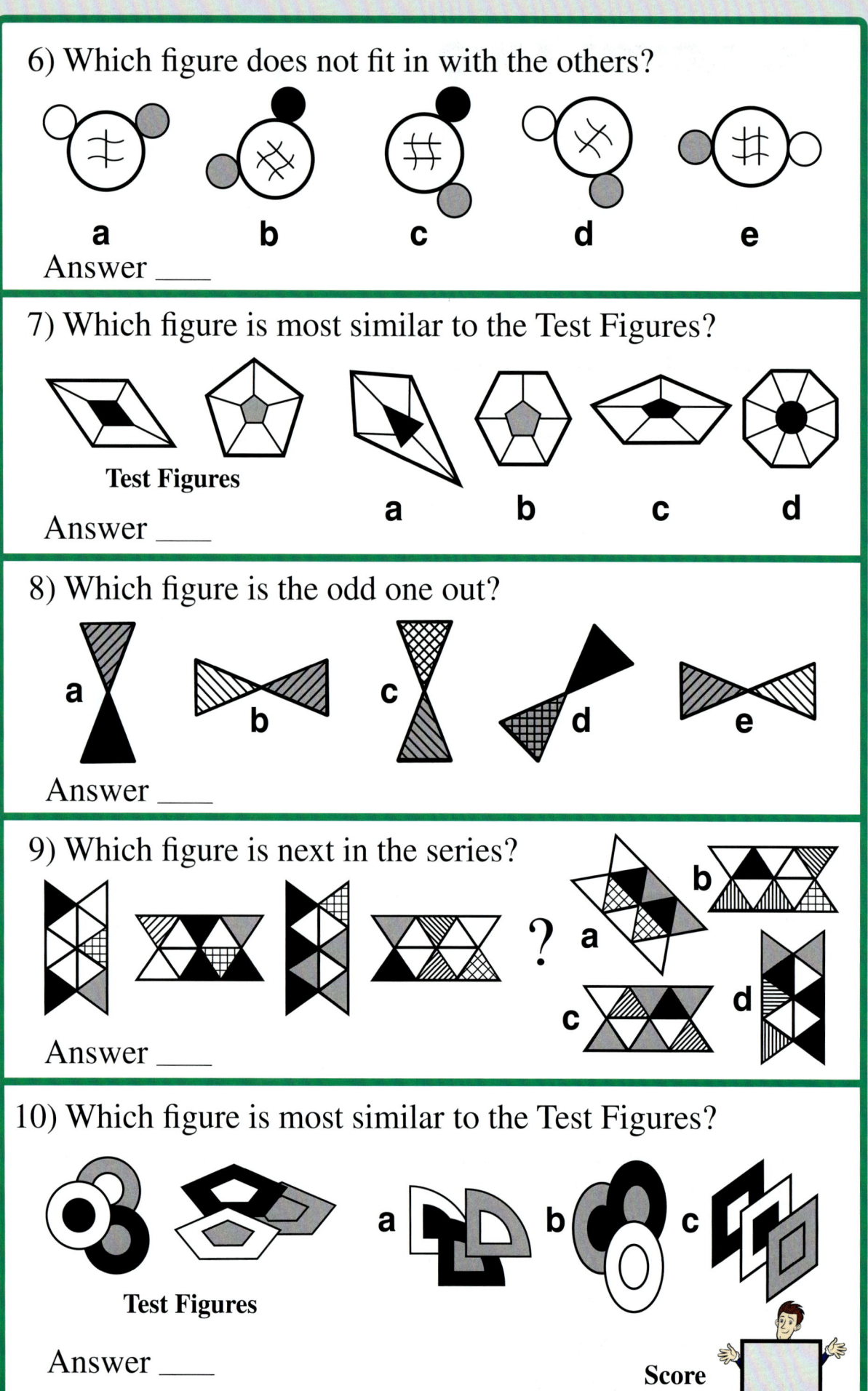

2. Level Two

In Non-verbal Reasoning, questions can have two layers:

Test Shape   Layer 1   Layer 2

The Pencil Shape has two layers (undergoes two changes):
Layer 1 - It has been reflected or rotated 180°.
Layer 2 - The Block Black Fill becomes a Block Grey Fill.

Example 1: Which shape completes the second pair of shapes?

                                   a   b   c   ⓓ

Answer: **d** - The shape enlarges and rotates 90° Anticlockwise (in the same way as the first pair).

Example 2: Which pair of shapes is the odd one out?

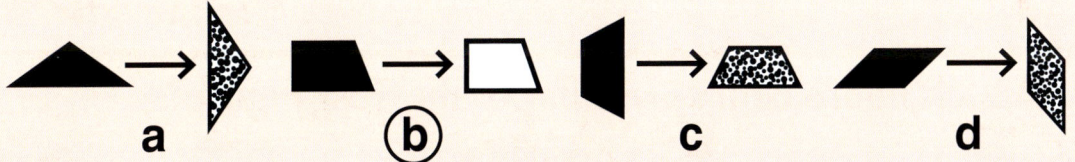

a   ⓑ   c   d

Answer: **b** does not rotate and has the wrong fill.

Example 3: Which figure is next in the series?

Answer: **a** has a Grey Fill (fills alternate) and it has a small Circle. (Pattern is two small Circles, then two large Circles, etc.)

Exercise 5: 2   Answer the following:

1) Which is the next figure in the series?

Answer ____

2) Which figure is most like the Test Figure?

Test Figure

Answer ____

3) Which is the next figure in the series?

Answer ____

4) Which figure is most similar to the Test Figure?

Test Figure

Answer ____

5) Which figure is next in the series?

Answer ____

6) Which two figures are most similar?

a b c d e

Answer ____ and ____

7) Which figure is most like the Test Figure?

Test Figure   a   b   c   d

Answer ____

8) Which figure is most similar to the Test Figure?

Test Figure   a   b   c   d

Answer ____

9) Which is the next figure in the series?

a b c d

Answer ____

10) Which figure is most like the Test Figure?

Test Figure   a   b   c   d

Answer ____

Score ____

3. Level Three

In Non-verbal Reasoning, questions can have three layers:

The Semi-circle has three layers (undergoes three changes):
Layer 1 - It has been rotated 180° or flipped Vertically.
Layer 2 - A Black Filled Bow Tie Shape is added at the top.
Layer 3 - A White Filled Star is added at the top.

Example 1: Which shape completes the second pair of shapes?

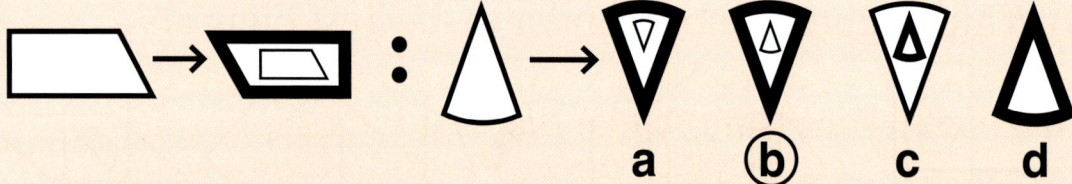

Answer: **b** - The outer shape rotates 180°; the line becomes thicker; a smaller but identical inner shape is enclosed within the outer shape.

Example 2: Which figure is the odd one out?

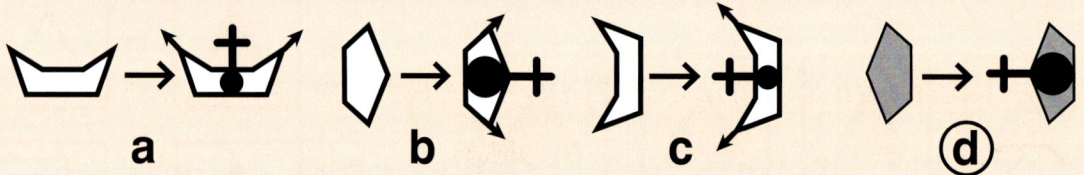

Answer: **d** - The Boat Shape should receive the three additions; **d** has a Circle with a Black Fill and a Black Cross Shape but no Arrow Shapes.

Example 3: Which figure is next in the series?

Answer: **c** - It has a Mottled Fill, both shapes rotate 90° Clockwise and the Ellipse reduces in size.

Exercise 5: 3   Answer the following:

1) Which is the next figure in the series?

Answer ____

2) Which figure is most similar to the Test Figure?

Test Figure   a   b   c   d

Answer ____

3) Which figure is most like the Test Figure?

Test Figure   a   b   c   d   e

Answer ____

4) Which figure completes the second pair of figures?

a   b   c   d

Answer ____

5) Which figure is most similar to the Test Figures?

Test Figures   a   b   c   d

Answer ____

6) Which figure is most like the Test Figure?

Test Figure   a   b   c   d

Answer ____

7) Which figure is most similar to the Test Figure?

Test Figure   a   b   c   d

Answer ____

8) Which is the next figure in the series?

a   b

c   d

Answer ____

9) Which figure is most similar to the Test Figure?

Test Figure   a   b   c   d

Answer ____

10) Which figure is most similar to the Test Figures?

Test Figures   a   b

c   d

Score

Answer ____

64   © 2006 Stephen Curran

4. Level Four

In Non-verbal Reasoning, questions can have four layers:

The Letter Shape has four layers (undergoes four changes):
Layer 1 - 'H' Shape rotated 90°.   **Layer 2** - 'H' Shape enlarged.
Layer 3 - Oval with a Grey Fill is added to the 'H' Shape.
Layer 4 - Blade Shape with a Liquid Fill is added to the 'H' Shape.

Example 1: Which figure completes the second pair of figures?

Answer: **b** - Shape rotates 90° Anticlockwise; figure enlarges; smaller identical inner shape with Black Fill added; Circle with Grey Fill added.

Example 2: Which pair of shapes is the odd one out?

Answer: **c** - Chevrons reflect or flip Horizontally; Diagonal Lines rotate 45° Clockwise; reflected shape gets larger but there is no Grey Fill.

Example 3: Which figure is next in the series?

Answer: **d** - One Circle transposes (moves) from Line to Line; one Line is added; the base enlarges; one more Line is added at the base.

© 2006 Stephen Curran

Exercise 5: 4   Answer the following:

1) Which is the next shape in the series?

Answer ____   a   b   c   d

2) Which figure is most similar to the Test Figure?

Answer ____   a   b   c   d   e

3) Which is the next figure in the series?

Answer ____

4) Which figure completes the second pair of figures?

Answer ____   a   b   c   d   e

5) Which is the next figure in the series?

Answer ____

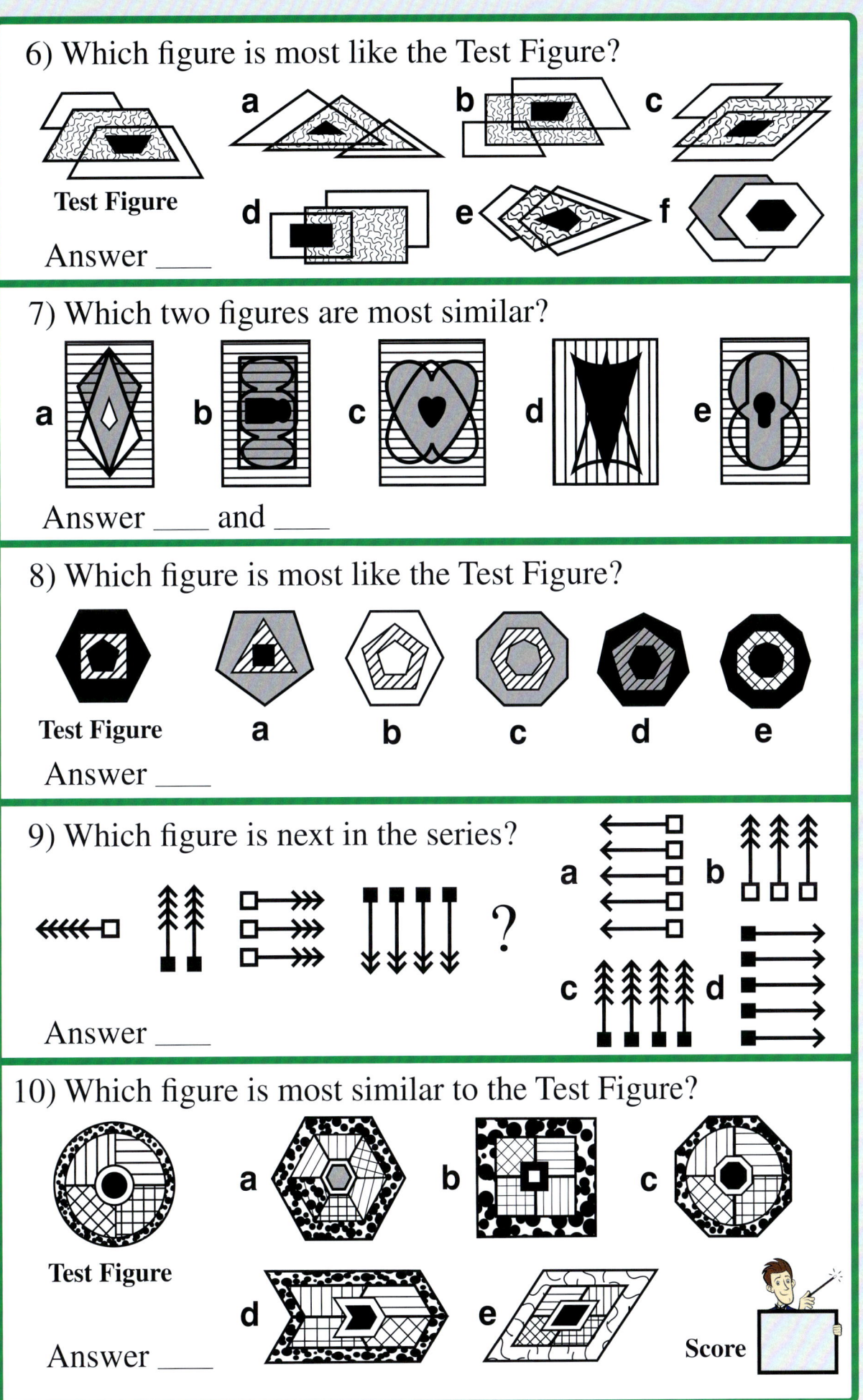

5. Level Five

In Non-verbal Reasoning, questions can have five layers:

The Flower Shape has five layers (undergoes five changes):
Layer 1 - Grey Filled Flower Shape is enclosed. **Layer 2** - Black Filled Cross is superimposed. **Layer 3** - Four Stars are superimposed.
Layer 4 - Four Arrows are added. **Layer 5** - Square encloses the shapes.

Example 1: Which figure completes the second pair of figures?

Answer: **b** - Two Rhombuses are added; the Rhombuses are reduced in size; all the Rhombuses are linked; the Pentagon is overlayed; the Black Filled Rhombus is enclosed.

Example 2: Which pair of figures is the odd one out?

Answer: **c** - The outer Pentagon rotates 180°; a Line Ending with a Circle is added; two Circles with Black Fills are added; a Thick Black Line is added but the Enclosed Pentagon with a Black Fill has not been rotated.

Example 3: Which figure is next in the series?

Answer: **a** - One of every shape is subtracted each time; all the shapes are flipped (reflected) Horizontally; the fills alternate between Black and White in the Squares; the Speaker Shapes rotate 90° Clockwise; one Arrow receives a Black Fill diagonally each time.

Exercise 5: 5   Answer the following:

1) Which is the next figure in the series?

Answer ____

2) Which figure is most similar to the Test Figure?

Test Figure   a   b   c   d   e

Answer ____

3) Which figure is most similar to the Test Figures?

Test Figures   a   b   c   d   e

Answer ____

4) Which figure is most like the Test Figure?

Test Figure   a   b   c   d

Answer ____

5) Which figure is most similar to the Test Figure?

Test Figure   a   b   c   d   e

Answer ____

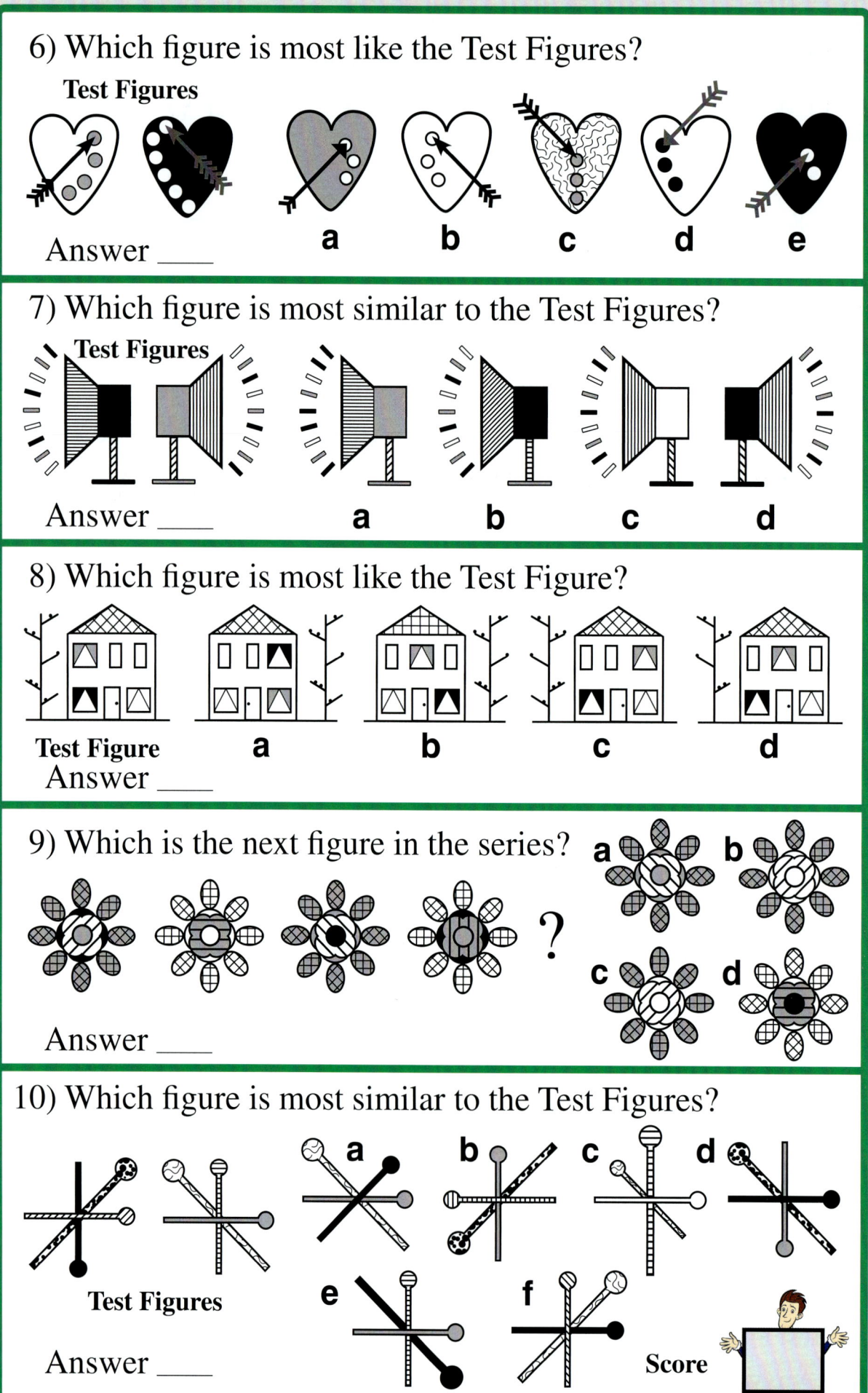

11+ Non-verbal Reasoning Year 5-7 Workbook 1

Answers

Chapter One
Elements
Exercise 1: 1
1) Quadrant
2) Arrowhead
3) Segment
4) Regular Octagon
5) Regular Hexagon
6) Trapezium
7) Ellipse
8) Parallelogram
9) Regular Nonagon
10) Scalene Triangle

Exercise 1: 2
1) Bone
2) Sea Horse
3) Speaker
4) Churn
5) Blade
6) Helmet
7) Boat
8) Flower
9) Wizard's Hat
10) Chevron

Exercise 1: 3
1) **b** - Regular Decagon
2) **c** - House/Irregular Pentagon
3) **b** - Ribbon or Flag
4) **e** - Straight Arrow
5) **b** - Equilateral Triangle
6) **d** - Helmet
7) **c** - Isosceles Triangle
8) **d** - Irregular Heptagon
9) **a** - Six-pointed Star
10) **c** - General Quadrilateral

Exercise 1: 4
1) Block/Grey
2) Cross-hatched/Lattice
3) Shaded/Vertical/Solid
4) Liquid/Speckled
5) Cross-hatched/Squares
6) Shaded/Left Slant/Dashed
7) Dotted/Close
8) Liquid/Mottled
9) Shaded/Horizontal/Dashed
10) Shaded/Right Slant/Solid

Exercise 1: 5
1) **a** - Block/Grey
2) **d** - Cross-hatched/Squares
3) **b** - Shaded/Horizontal/Solid
4) **d** - Shaded/Vertical/Solid
5) **b** - Liquid/Mottled
6) **b/e** - Liquid/Speckled
7) **c** - Shaded/Left Slant/Dashed
8) **b** - Block/Black
9) **b** - Cross-hatched/Lattice
10) **e** - Liquid/Speckled

Exercise 1: 6a
1) Dotted/Straight/Thin; Cross.
2) Solid/Straight/Thick; Symbol.
3) Dashed/Straight/Thin; Pitchfork.
4) Dashed/Straight/Thin; Letter.
5) Solid/Straight/Thin; Zigzag.

Exercise 1: 6b
6) Dashed/Curved/Thin; Wave.
7) Solid/CurvedThick; Fish.
8) Solid/Curved/Thin; Pulleys.
9) Dotted/Curved/Thin; Curved Arrow.
10) Solid/Curved/Thick; Basin.

Exercise 1: 7
1) **b** - Telegraph Poles
2) **c** - Straight Arrows
3) **b** - Grille
4) **c** - Symbol
5) **d** - Curved Arrow
6) **d** - Solid/Straight/Thick
7) **b** - Dashed/Curved/Thin
8) **e** - Dotted/Straight/Thin
9) **b** - Symbols
10) **b** - Dotted/Straight/Thin

Exercise 1: 8
1) **a** - The order of fills is: Grey, Black, White.
2) **b** - It is rotated at 45° or Diagonally, whereas the others are positioned either Vertically or Horizontally.
3) **c** - The fills alternate Grey/Dotted/Grey and the sides lessen by two each time.
4) **d** - It only has five sides whereas all the other shapes have six sides.
5) **d** - The shape rotates 180° each time and the shading rotates 45° Clockwise each time.
6) **c** and **e** - The shapes have Slanted Shading.
7) **c** - It has a Black Fill whereas the others have either White or Grey Fills.
8) **b** - It has an odd number of sides like the Test Shape.
9) **a** - The Star Shape must be smaller with a Liquid (Mottled) Fill.
10) **a** - It is a standard, one-sided Circular Shape like the Test Shape.

© 2006 Stephen Curran

Answers

11+ Non-verbal Reasoning Year 5-7 Workbook 1

Chapter Two
Movements
Exercise 2: 1
1) **b** - Shaded/Right Slanted Solid
2) **d** - Chevrons
3) **a** - Liquid/Speckled and Mottled
4) **d** - It is a Helmet and not a Shield.
5) **c** - M is the next letter that has a Reflective Line of Symmetry.
6) **a** and **d** - Both pairs of shapes reflect.
7) **e** - i) The shapes reflect. ii) Ribbons or Flags
8) **b** - Blade
9) **a** - Sector
10) **b** - Bean

Exercise 2: 2
1) **b** - 45°; Anticlockwise.
2) **b** - 180°
3) **a** - 90° Clockwise
4) **c** - 90° and 180°
5) **d** - Clockwise
6) **e** - The shading goes in the same direction.
7) **c** - The Arrow goes in a Clockwise direction.
8) **c** - 180°
9) **b** - 45°; 90°; Anticlockwise.
10) **a** - The letter F only rotates once (360°).

Exercise 2: 3
1) **a** - Vertical inversion or flip.
2) **b** - It is an inversion; the other shapes are rotations.
3) **d** - Horizontal and Vertical inversion (rotated 180°).
4) **a** - It can only be seen as a Horizontal inversion, whereas the others are all 180° rotations.
5) **c** - It rotates 90°, has a Grey Fill and is inverted Horizontally.
6) **a** and **c** - They match as rotations, whereas the others are inversions.
7) **c** - All the letters have been rotated 180° (double flipped), but the letter F is a Vertical inversion.
8) **d** - It is an inversion of the Test Shape and will not rotate.
9) **d** - The pattern is a Vertical inversion or flip, then reflection, etc; The order of fills is: Shading, Shading, Liquid (Mottled).
10) **c** - It is the only Horizontally inverted or flipped figure.

Exercise 2: 4
1) **c** - Merger
2) **e** - Overlay
3) **a** - Linkage
4) **b** - Enclosure
5) **d** - Overlay
6) **c** - Merger/Linkage
7) **d** - Enclosure
8) **c** - Merger
9) **b** - Overlay
10) **b** - Overlay/Linkage/Enclosure

Exercise 2: 5
1) **d** - Grey Fill/Horizontal; White Fill/Vertical; Black Fill/Horizontal.
2) **a** - Flower/Horizontal; Curved Arrow/Vertical; Circle/Vertical.
3) **d** - Circle/Vertical; Pentagon/Horizontal.
4) **c** - Horizontal and Vertical
5) **b** - Octagon/Vertical; Kite/Horizontal.
6) **b** - Curved Arrow/Horizontal; F Shape/Vertical and Horizontal.
7) **d** - Horizontal
8) **a** - Black Shape/Horizontal; Grey Shape/Vertical.
9) **d** - Vertical
10) **b** - Vertical and Horizontal

Chapter Three
Manipulations
Exercise 3: 1
1) **b** - Enlargement
2) **c** - Reduction
3) **d** - Arrow/Reduces Heart/Enlarges
4) **c** - Reduction
5) **b** - Reduction
6) **d** - Enlargement
7) **a** - Reduction
8) **d** - Reduction
9) **c** - Enlargement
10) **a** - Reduction

Exercise 3: 2
1) **d** - Squashed
2) **c** - Stretched
3) **c** - House Shape Stretched; Cross Shape Squashed.
4) **b** - Hexagon
5) **a** - Square
6) **b** and **e** - Stretched
7) **d** - Squashed
8) **b** - Squashed
9) **d** - Stretched
10) **c** - Squashed/Left Stretched/Right

11+ Non-verbal Reasoning Year 5-7 Workbook 1

Answers

Exercise 3: 3
1) **a** - Isosceles Trapezium
2) **d** - Parallelogram
3) **c** - Speaker
4) **b** - Flower
5) **c** - Two shapes
6) **d** - Black Fill
7) **c** - One shape
8) **a** - Three Ellipses have been added instead of two.
9) **b** - White/Grey/Black/White
10) **b** - i) Rotates 90°
    ii) Next letter in the alphabet.
    iii) Square has a Grey Fill.

Exercise 3: 4
1) **a** - Line/Anticlockwise
2) **c** - i) An enclosed shape.
    ii) A Horizontal Shaded Fill.
3) **a** - i) An Arrowhead.
    ii) The fill gets lighter.
4) **d** - The wrong Diagonal Line has been subtracted on the Square.
5) **a** - Vertical then Horizontal.
6) **a** and **c** - i) A quarter of the shape is subtracted.
    ii) The fill is subtracted and replaced by a White Fill.
7) **c** - Two shapes with Grey Fills must be subtracted.
8) **c** - i) The Shaded Fill.
    ii) The outer shape with a Dashed Line.
9) **b** - Circle with a White Fill.
10) **a** - i) One merged shape.
    ii) The smallest enclosed shape.

Exercise 3: 5
1) **c** - 8, 1, 6, 3, 4, 5
2) **a** - A Five-pointed Star with a White Fill has replaced a Cross with a White Fill. It now has six Five-pointed Stars rather than five.
3) **b** - Four enclosures
4) **c** - Five H Letters
5) **b** - There must be two of each type of Cross.
6) **b** - One of the Shields with a Black Fill should have a Grey Fill.
7) **c** - Two less sides.
8) **e** - Four of each.
9) **d** - 4, 3, 6, 5, 8, 7
10) **c** - The three shapes must have a consecutive number of sides, e.g. 5, 6, 7 sides, etc.

Chapter Four
Patterns
Exercise 4: 1
1) **a** - 1, 2, 3, 2, 1, etc.
2) **a** - Anticlockwise
3) **d** - Reflection
4) **d** - White/Grey Mottled/White
5) **c** - Shaded Fill/Right Slanted Solid Line
6) **c** - 6, 5, 3, 5, 6
7) **b** - Five-pointed Star
8) **a** - White/Black/Grey/White/Black, etc.
9) **b** - Each shape changes size in the order: small, medium, large, small, etc.
10) **a** - Black Fill rotates Clockwise; Grey Fill rotates Anticlockwise.

Exercise 4: 2
1) **b** - Heart, Churn, Bulb
2) **a** - Dashed, Straight and Thin; Solid, Straight and Thick.
3) **b** - Rhombus
4) **c** - Flower Shape
5) **d** - Add a Solid Line; subtract Phone Shape.
6) **c** - A Circle with a Block Black Fill.
7) **d** - i) Solid Line gets thinner.
    ii) The Black Fill is replaced by a White Fill in the Squares.
8) **c** - One Arrowhead.
9) **a** - A Semi-circle with a Speckled Fill.
10) **c** - Squares fill sequence: Grey/Black/White/Grey; cumulative action: Triangles and Circles enlarge.

Chapter Five
Layering
Exercise 5: 1
1) **c** - The figure squashes.
2) **b** - The shape does not have a Cross-hatched Fill.
3) **c** - The outer shape has a Grey Fill.
4) **d** - The line ending has White Fill.
5) **c** - The shape is not a rotation of the other shapes.
6) **e** - The smaller Circles are not in the same position as they are in the other figures.
7) **c** - The enclosed shape is the same as the outer shape.
8) **d** - The figure does not have a Shaded Fill.

11+ Non-verbal Reasoning Year 5-7 Workbook 1

Answers

9) **d** - The figure alternates between vertical and horizontal positioning.
10) **b** - The figure with the White Outer Fill overlays the other two figures.

Exercise 5: 2
1) **c** - The Bean Shape rotates 45° anticlockwise and the Grey Fill gets darker.
2) **b** - The Comb Shape and the Shaded Fill is the same as in the Test Figure.
3) **b** - The Circle moves one position anticlockwise and the fill alternates between Black and White.
4) **c** - From back to front, the order of size of the overlay is: large, small, large. The order of fills is: Grey, Black, Shaded.
5) **a** - The number of Chevron Shapes is: 2, 4, 3, 2, 4. The positioning of the Chevron Shapes is: bottom, middle, top, bottom, middle.
6) **a** and **d** - The outer shape has a Lattice Fill. The enclosed Squares are the same size.
7) **b** - The shapes have a background with a White Fill and the same Shaded Fill.
8) **c** - The enclosed shape has one less side than the larger shapes. The enclosed shape has a Grey Fill.
9) **a** - The Arrow rotates 90° clockwise. The outline of the Triangle increases in thickness.

10) **d** - The central Line is a line of symmetry. One half of the shape has a Black Fill and one half of the shape has a Grey Fill.

Exercise 5: 3
1) **d** - The fill of the Square alternates between Left Slant Shaded and Right Slant Shaded. The fill of the Arrow alternates between Horizontal Shaded and Vertical Shaded. The Arrow alternates between pointing upwards and pointing downwards.
2) **d** - The largest shape is Straight-edged. The enclosed shape has a Left Slant Shaded Fill. The small overlaid shape has a White Fill; the medium overlaid shape has a Grey Fill; the large overlaid shape has a Black Fill.
3) **c** - There are four of the same shape. The order of fills is: Black, White, Grey, Lattice. The enclosed shape is a 180° rotation of the outer shape.
4) **c** - The outer shape becomes the central enclosed shape. The central enclosed shape becomes the outer shape. The Black Fill moves outwards one position.
5) **b** - There is a Set Square Shape with a White Fill enclosed in a Curved Shape with a Black Fill. The outer shape has a Grey or White Fill.

6) **a** - The figure is horizontal. One row of Squares contains one Circle with a White Fill, one Black Fill and one Cross. One row of Squares contains one Cross with a 45° rotation, one Triangle with a Grey Fill, and one Circle with a Black Fill.
7) **b** - The top and bottom shapes are the same and the left and right shapes are the same. The adjacent fills are the same. One enclosed shape has a Black Fill and one enclosed shape has a White Fill.
8) **c** - The Black and White Fills swap. The shapes move one position anticlockwise. The sizes and fills stay in the same position.
9) **d** - The figure has two Wheel Shapes. The enclosed shape with a White Fill and a shape with a Grey Fill face the same way. The shape with a Black Fill is flipped vertically.
10) **b** - The enclosed Ribbon Shapes have different fills. The left and right Ribbon Shapes have either the same fill or reflecting fills. The middle Ribbon Shape has a White Fill if one of the enclosed Ribbon Shapes has a White Fill, or has a Mottled Fill if one of the enclosed Ribbon Shapes has a Black Fill.

Answers

11+ Non-verbal Reasoning Year 5-7 Workbook 1

Exercise 5: 4

1) **a** - The Boot Shape reflects horizontally. The fills alternate between Grey and White. The enclosed Shaded Fill becomes more condensed. The outline alternates between Thick and Thin.

2) **d** - The Circle has a Black Fill. The Cigar Shape has a Dashed Shaded Fill. The central enclosed Triangle has a Black Fill. The middle enclosed Triangle has a Dashed Outline.

3) **a** - The Triangle with a Black Fill and an enclosed Triangle with a White Fill move one position clockwise, overlaying the fill in that space. The enclosed Triangle flips. The Shaded Fill alternates between Vertical and Horizontal. The Cross-hatched Fill alternates between Lattice and Squares.

4) **c** - There are two enclosed Hexagons opposite each other, and two enclosed Pentagons opposite each other. The Black and White Fills of the Hexagons swap. The Pentagon with a White Fill becomes Grey. The Grey Square becomes Black.

5) **c** - The enclosed Square alternates between large and small. The order of fills of the outer Square is: Black, Grey, White, Black, Grey. The order of fills of the enclosed Square is: Grey, White, Black, Grey, White. The order of Shaded Fills of the enclosed Circle is: Horizontal, Right Slant, Vertical, Left Slant, Horizontal.

6) **e** - There are two large shapes, one medium shape and one small shape. The large shapes link. The small shape has a Black Fill, is flipped and is enclosed in the linkage. One large shape has a Mottled Fill and overlays the medium shape.

7) **c** and **e** - The Rectangle has a Horizontal Shaded Fill. The large enclosed shapes are the same, but face in opposite directions, and are merged. One of the enclosed shapes has a Grey Fill and the other enclosed shape has a White Fill. The central enclosed shape is the same shape as the larger two and has a Black Fill.

8) **c** - The middle shape has two less sides than the outer shape. The central enclosed shape has one less side than the outer shape. The outer and central shapes have the same fill. The middle shape has a Right Slant Shaded Fill.

9) **a** - One figure is added and one Arrowhead is removed. The figure rotates 90° clockwise. The fill of the Square line ending alternates between Black and White.

10) **d** - There are four similar shapes enclosing each other. The outer shape has a Speckled Fill. The second shape is split into quarters. The third shape has a White Fill and overlays the fills of the second shape. The central shape has a Black Fill.

Exercise 5: 5

1) **d** - The figure rotates 45° clockwise. The order of superimpositons of the smaller Sectors is: merger, overlay, linkage, overlay, merger. The fill of the smaller Sector alternates between Black and White. The Shaded Fills swap. The figure alternates between large and small.

2) **d** - The outer border has a Black Fill. The fill of the enclosed Circle is Right Slant Shaded. There are two Stars enclosed. One Star has a Grey Fill and one Star has a White Fill. The smaller Star has two points less than the larger Star.

11+ Non-verbal Reasoning Year 5-7 Workbook 1

Answers

3) **b** - There are two Arrows. The Arrow with the Block Fill points to the Circle. The Circle has a different Block Fill from the Block Fill of the Arrow. The other Arrow has a Left Slant Shaded Fill. If the Arrow has a Black Fill, it overlays the Shaded Arrow; if the Arrow has a White Fill, the two Arrows are merged.

4) **d** - The Churn Shape faces right. The three Quadrants at each end face inwards towards the Lines. The three Quadrants at the base of the Churn Shape have the same fill as the middle Quadrant at the top of the Churn Shape. The central fill is a different Block Fill from the Block Fill of the Quadrants. The Churn Shape has a Thick Outline.

5) **e** - There is one small and one large Cigar Shape. The small Cigar Shape overlays the large Cigar Shape. The small Cigar Shape has a Black Fill; the large Cigar Shape has a Dashed Shaded Fill. The two Cigar Shapes are perpendicular to each other.

6) **b** - The Heart Shape has a Black Fill or White Fill. The Circles have a Grey Fill or White Fill. The number of Circles equals the number of Arrow line endings. The Arrow points upwards. The Arrowhead is Curved.

7) **d** - The small Rectangles have Block Fills in the following order: White, Grey, Black. The Rectangles at the top and base of the figure have the same fill, which is Black or Grey. The vertical Rectangle has a Right Slant Shaded Fill. The Isosceles Trapezium has a Vertical or Horizontal Shaded Fill.

8) **c** - There are seven small Circles on five lines as a tree. The roof has a Lattice Fill. One window has curtains with a Black Fill, one window has curtains with a White Fill and one window has curtains with a Grey Fill. There are two Rectangle windows. The Circle is on the right of the door.

9) **b** - The Ellipses alternate between Grey with a Lattice Fill and White with a Squares Fill. The order of fills of the larger Flower Shape is: Black, White, Grey, Black, White. The order of Block Fills of the enclosed Flower Shape alternates between White and Grey. The shaded fill of the enclosed Flower Shape rotates 45° clockwise. The order of fills of the enclosed Circle is: Grey, White, Black, Grey, White.

10) **b** - There are three Matchstick Shapes. Two of the Matchstick Shapes are the same size - one is vertical and one is horizontal; the other Matchstick Shape is larger and diagonal. One of the smaller Matchstick Shapes has a Block Fill; the other has a Shaded Fill. The larger Matchstick Shape has a Liquid Fill.

PROGRESS CHARTS

1. ELEMENTS

Exercises

2. MOVEMENTS

Exercises

3. MANIPULATIONS

Exercises

4. PATTERNS

Scores

5. LAYERING

Exercises

Shade in your score for each exercise on the graphs. Add up for your total score.

For the average add up % and divide by 5

Overall Percentage

%

CERTIFICATE OF ACHIEVEMENT

This certifies

_____

has successfully completed

11+ Non-verbal Reasoning
Year 5–7
WORKBOOK 1

Overall percentage score achieved ☐ %

Comment _____

_____

Signed _____
(teacher/parent/guardian)

Date _____